Angel of Death

Life of Serial Killer Donald Harvey

Jack Smith

Copyrights

All rights reserved. © Jack Smith (2017) and Maplewood Publishing (2017). No part of this publication or the information in it may be quoted from or reproduced in any form by means such as printing, scanning, photocopying, or otherwise without prior written permission of the copyright holder.

Disclaimer and Terms of Use

Effort has been made to ensure that the information in this book is accurate and complete. However, the author and the publisher do not warrant the accuracy of the information, text, and graphics contained within the book due to the rapidly changing nature of science, research, known and unknown facts, and internet. The author and the publisher do not hold any responsibility for errors, omissions, or contrary interpretation of the subject matter herein. This book is presented solely for motivational and informational purposes only.

Warning

Throughout the book there are some descriptions of murders and crime scenes that some people might find disturbing. There are also language used by people involved in the murders that may not be appropriate.

ISBN: 978-1717419644

Printed in the United States

MAPLEWOOD
— PUBLISHING —

Contents

Early Life 1
   The Birth of the Angel 3
   Education and Adolescence 7
Start of the Descent 11
   The Angel at Work 13
   Personal Life 19
   The First Kill 27
The Serial Killer 29
   The Victims 31
   The Investigation and Guilty Plea 45
   The Confession and Sentence 53
The Final End 55
   Testimonials 57
   The Death of the Angel and Similar Cases 61
Epilogue 65
Also by Jack Smith 67

Early Life

Childhood experiences have both overt and covert effects on adult life. An abusive childhood, for example, will develop in an individual a strong sense of self-preservation and self-defense. The same childhood can emotionally scar the individual by lowering his or her self-confidence and self-esteem. To truly understand Donald Harvey, therefore, the first step is to look into his childhood experiences.

From a young age, Donald lived a life of abuse and trauma. There was not a moment of peace in his childhood. He lived in a hostile environment, where his parents were always fighting, and he was raped by his uncle, a neighbor, and—later on—his roommate. Eventually, he got tired of being boxed in. His life was a series of bad situations without any foreseeable escape route.

There is no denying that Donald Harvey was dealt a bad hand. Life threw horrible experiences his way like curveballs—expected yet unpredictable. Does that justify becoming a serial killer? Was getting back at Fate an appropriate response to all its offenses against him? Perhaps no one can truly judge Donald Harvey as an individual—but here is the story of his childhood.

The Birth of the Angel

According to adults, Donald Harvey was a very well-behaved boy. His teachers commended him for being quiet, gentle, and cheerful. His classmates, however, did not appreciate these traits quite as much. Many of them saw him as an unapproachable loner due to the same quietness that his teachers praised.

Studies conducted at Toin University of Yokohama have shown that certain childhood experiences increase the chances of becoming a serial killer—and Donald Harvey had them.

In October of 1952, a mere six months after he was born, his father accidentally dropped him on his head. Ray Harvey was rocking his little boy back and forth, trying to put him to sleep, but he was tired himself and ended up falling asleep first. Upon entering the room, Goldie Harvey took one look at her fallen, crying child and started screaming at her husband. The rudely awoken Ray got angry too, and in the ensuing argument no one thought to check on Donald's head injury. It does not seem to have been serious, but this incident created a rift between his parents that would never close.

Instead of putting it behind her, Goldie reported this story to the newspapers. When her husband saw the reports, he felt betrayed by his wife, and although he still loved her, things were never the same afterwards. As the first of three children, Donald experienced the brunt of the hostile environment. His parents would hurt each other and shout at each other, and sadly, the little boy often found himself in the middle of their squabbles.

Ray and Goldie continued their abusive relationship for years. While the couple still loved each other, they were no longer happy together. They stayed together for the sake of their children, apparently without understanding how damaging their discord was to the psyches of the kids they so wanted to protect. They were also neglectful, and Donald grew up without knowing what a peaceful, loving home was like.

Unbeknownst to his parents, he was also being sexually abused by his uncle, cousins, and a neighbor. One day, after Goldie had dropped off the little boy at her mother's house, his Uncle Wayne set his eyes on him. Goldie's half-brother, Uncle Wayne was a trusted member of the family, and no one ever thought that he would do what he did to little Donald.

At the young age of four, Donald experienced his first sexual encounter. His uncle used him as a tool for masturbation, asking for hand jobs whenever they were together at Donald's grandmother's home. Being the innocent child that he was, Donald did not find anything wrong with following his uncle's orders. Then, after getting away with enjoying a few hand jobs and other sexual favors, Wayne became brazen. He decided that Donald was ready to perform oral sex.

His uncle started training him to become the perfect toy for his own pleasure, and Donald had no choice but to endure the abuse—without really knowing that he was being abused. His mother and father were too preoccupied trying to keep their marriage together to notice that anything was wrong. And a year later, little Donald caught the eye of another man with ill intentions.

Dan Thomas was the Harveys' neighbor, and he saw the way that Uncle Wayne would look at Donald. It did not take him long to conceive a plan to use the little boy himself. On an unremarkable afternoon, when Ron and Goldie were otherwise occupied, Dan invited Donald into his home. Donald did not see anything wrong with visiting a neighbor, so he accepted the invitation.

Inside the older man's home, Donald experienced the same things he had with his uncle—and more. Donald found himself escaping from one abusive home to another. To get away from his parents' screaming and fighting, he would go to Dan's house. Dan taught him all sorts of inappropriate things—things that no 5-year-old child should experience. When Donald later recalled this abuse, he confided that he'd liked that his neighbor paid him from time to time.

As further proof of neglect, in the same year that Dan began to abuse him, Donald got another head injury. He was standing on the running board of a truck when he slipped and fell on his head. He received a four-inch gash on the back of his scalp as a result of this mishap. While this injury was treated properly, all of his other, less obvious injuries had gone unnoticed.

It is no wonder that Donald felt constricted and controlled. He was stuck between two older men who saw him as a sexual stimulant rather than a child. When he was not being sexually abused, he was forced to stay in a home where his parents were screaming obscenities at each other almost daily and even resorting to physical force at times. Day and night, little Donald was surrounded by molesters, pedophiles, and abusers. He grew up thinking that such maltreatment was normal—and what was normal, of course, was okay.

Some say that, given his childhood, it was almost inevitable that Donald would become a serial killer. His childhood was a blend of sexual abuse and parental neglect, devoid of care and love. So as not to call attention to himself, Donald quickly learned to hide his emotions and remain stoic and expressionless. Because of his less-than-ideal childhood, Donald grew up different from the other kids. When other kids were loud and conspicuous, he was quiet and observant. While others were playing and having fun, Donald kept to himself and learned to amuse himself in his own way. While his teachers found him brilliant and well-behaved, the other children found him queer.

At the time, no one knew just how badly the trauma was affective Donald's state of mind. Because he was so good at hiding his emotions and redirecting attention, no one imagined that this little child was thinking of how he could escape his current predicament—using any means possible. And if his early childhood was a series of horrendous events, his formative years and adolescence were just as horrendous, if not more so.

Education and Adolescence

Donald's uncle and neighbor continued their abuse until he was twenty. Whenever Donald visited his grandmother, Wayne would quietly usher him into his room for some service. Eventually, Donald became the perfect toy, and his uncle was well satisfied. At the same time, Dan was also making use of Donald's talents in the bedroom for his own pleasure. The two older men did not stop, and eventually Donald came to enjoy the experience—even as he came to realize that what they were doing to him was wrong.

The decade of abuse shifted the boy's perception of normal and abnormal. What was normal to him was abnormal to others. On Donald's first day of kindergarten in Bourneville, Kentucky, his mother and father dropped him off together. To everyone there, they looked like a happy family—even though Goldie was concealing a black eye from the most recent quarrel. From youth to adulthood, Donald rarely showed his emotions, and this occasion was no different. While most of the kids cried when their parents left, Donald merely stared at his parents' retreating figures, not even batting an eyelash.

While most people saw Donald as an unremarkable child, he was quite different. In a room full of people, he was always the one who kept to himself while the others were mingling. His silence was seen as good behavior, and his parents were proud that their son was such a good student. While other students were busy wreaking havoc on the school, Donald stayed silently in his chair waiting for the day to end.

Because of his experiences, Donald knew not to call attention to himself. He never created a fuss, and he never caused trouble for his teachers. He was a model student, and his parents were happy to take the credit for his attitude. As a student, no one could fault him. He got good grades, never put a toe out of line, and always made sure to greet his teachers. But as Donald was an exceptionally intelligent child, he found high school dull and uninformative, and he soon dropped out. Despite this, he received his diploma from Chicago's long-distance American School when he was 16, and his GED the year after.

Donald entered adolescence highly skeptical of adults and of the world in general. While he was a model student, he did not do as well with his personal relationships. In the same year that he got his diploma and GED, Donald also started his first romantic relationship, with James Peluso. Abuse did not figure in their on-again, off-again relationship; rather, Donald and James were equal and everything was consensual.

This relationship was to last for 15 years, but Donald remained a willing participant in the perversions of his uncle and neighbor. He was now aware of the abnormality involved, but he had become used to what he did with Wayne and Dan in their bedrooms. Whenever they called on him, he would still do their bidding willingly—that Dan paid him was only a bonus.

Donald learned to maintain neutral expressions and hide his emotions. He became calm and composed—and eventually manipulative. He quickly became an adept actor, because he had to pretend that nothing was wrong even when his entire life was a jumble of mishaps and abuses. He was used to painting himself as the victim, and he was able to force others to think that way as well. His experience in life taught him that no one was to be trusted, and therefore everyone must be manipulated. Once Donald had learned this lesson, his controlled life—a life where people and circumstance dictated his every move—became a little more free.

From his first taste of control, Donald wanted more. He had a need for control that had to be sated, and so he started to further develop his manipulating skills. His relationship with James was an occasional one only because he wanted it to be so. Instead of admitting this to James outright, he bided his time, enjoying manipulating his partner into feeling that all he wanted was a fling, a passing chance that might or might not be repeated. This allowed him two things: freedom and convenience.

He had the freedom to have other partners, as evidenced by his continued relationships with Dan Thomas and Uncle Wayne. He did not need to explain to James why he was seeing two other men. Moreover, he had the freedom to say "yes" and "no" whenever he pleased, and he was not committed to James in any way. The relationship was romantic, yes, but no commitments were made. And in this sense, Donald was free—freer than he had ever been in any other relationship.

The open-ended nature of the relationship made life in general much more convenient, too. Donald kept his options open; he did not need to explain to James that he was going to move to a different state. Meanwhile, he could ask James for sexual favors whenever he wanted to. As Donald and James were theoretically equal partners in the relationship, their sexual encounters were enjoyable rather than abusive.

However, what James didn't realize was that Donald was using their relationship to hone his skills in manipulation and coercion. He was able to trick James into wanting things that he wanted, and also into thinking that it was all his plan—when in reality, Donald was the mastermind of everything.

During this stage of Donald's life, freedom became a big issue. Freedom and control were two fundamental rights that were missing in his formative years. This lack made him want them that much more, so the first thing he did after getting his GED was to look for a job that would get him out of his sorry predicament.

His first job was in a factory. It wasn't difficult, and while he didn't enjoy the work, he did reap the benefits of working hard, earning enough to support himself and then some. And he was already planning his next move. He was going to move out. Nothing and no one could stop him.

He was laid off shortly after he was hired, but not before he had saved enough money for the move. So at the age of 18, in the year 1970, Donald moved to London, Kentucky. He had no drive, no ambition, and no plan—all he knew was that he needed to start living life for himself, by his own rules. His parents could not stop him from leaving, and Donald was glad to get away from the cold, abusive environment in which he grew up.

Once in Kentucky, he landed a job as a nursing assistant at Marymount Hospital. But while Donald thought that things were about to get better, he could not have been any more wrong.

Start of the Descent

Donald had an abusive childhood, and during his school years this made him reserved and contemplative—he rarely showed emotion and even more rarely asked for help. His experiences had forced him to become stoic and neutral. He barely interacted with his classmates and, while his teachers were proud of his behavior, he was seen as weird and unapproachable.

But that all changed once he saved up enough to leave home. He had always been intelligent, and as he matured he became ever more adept at manipulation. He remained soft-spoken, but he adopted a friendlier manner, charming his way into one job after another and getting along well with his coworkers. On the surface, Donald seemed to have put his horrific past behind him. There a few minor brushes with the law, an unusual fascination with the occult, but by and large he became a reasonably solid citizen.

Except, of course, for the murders.

The Angel at Work

Over the course of seventeen years, Donald worked for various health institutions. The first of these was Marymount Hospital in London, Kentucky.

Donald had chosen to go to London because his grandfather lived there. The old man was sick, and he figured he could care for him and keep him company. He would go to Marymount Hospital daily to spend time with his grandfather. Over time, he became friends with the nurses and doctors. He was such a frequent visitor that almost everyone recognized him, and it was not long before he was offered a job as an orderly.

His responsibilities brought him closer to the patients. He was in charge of administering medicine, inserting catheters, bathing the elderly, and taking care of other medical needs. He learned the ropes quickly and soon became among the most adept orderlies in the hospital. Just as he'd been the model student, he was also a model employee. He was precise, agile, and hardworking.

He interacted with his patients on a daily basis, and no one complained about his performance. His colleagues saw him as a reliable and qualified addition to the team. What they did not know was that his daily interactions with patients gave him a sense of control that was lacking in the rest of his life. Donald Harvey, the boy who'd had no control over his parents' quarrels or his sexual abuse, was now a man who suddenly had control over other people—and it was empowering.

During his time at the Marymount hospital, Donald had a roommate named Randy White. And although he was already an adult, he had no power against Randy. Donald was a handsome lad, and Randy was attracted him. It did not take long before

Randy wanted more than just a roommate relationship. As Donald was unaware of the feelings the other youth harbored for him, he did not see it coming when Randy finally made his move—and raped him.

Donald was in shock. He could not do anything to stop Randy from taking what he wanted and having his way with him. While the emotional scars of being abused as a child ran deep, new wounds opened when he was raped as an adult. Now he was fully aware of his powerlessness. No one knows what finally pushed him over the edge, but shortly after this incident, Donald made his first kill—and fourteen more after that.

On March 27, 1971, Donald resigned from his post at Marymount Hospital. His reasons are unknown. Three days after his resignation, Donald was arrested for the first time. He was tired, at loose ends, and did not know what to do. He decided to go to a local bar and get as drunk as he could. While intoxicated, he robbed his apartment building, and was immediately arrested for burglary.

While he was still drunk, the police questioned him relentlessly, both about the burglary and about the occult materials in his possession. Finally losing his cool, Donald confessed to murdering fifteen people at Marymount Hospital. The police were shocked at the revelation—and skeptical. Here was a drunken man, with no criminal record, telling them that he had murdered fifteen people.

They investigated the matter anyway, but found no evidence to support his claims. When he went to court, he was merely charged with petty theft and made to pay a small fine.

The judge who tried this case recommended that Donald receive psychiatric treatment, but on June 16 he enlisted in the Air Force instead. He completed basic training, but left the service prematurely nine months later. The reasons for this are unclear, but he was granted an honorable discharge. While no one knew what had motivated Donald to enlist in the first place, when he was discharged, everyone knew that there was something wrong.

After leaving the Air Force, Donald went back to Kentucky—not happily, it seems. He had a bout of depression bad enough that he spent a month in the V.A. hospital on two separate occasions—July 16 to August 25, and then again from September 17 to October 17 of 1972. He received various treatments, but was ultimately released without being cured.

After his stint with the Air Force and his stays at the V.A. hospital, Donald embarked on a series of jobs in various places around Kentucky—and for two years, he was able to subdue his urge to kill. He first found work at the Cardinal Hill Convalescent Hospital as a part-time nurse's aide, starting in February of 1973. From June of that year he also worked part-time for the Good Samaritan Hospital in Lexington.

By August of 1974, he changed his line of work, becoming a telephone operator for a year. He then returned to the healthcare field as a clerk at St. Luke's Medical Hospital. Still unsatisfied with his job, he decided that he needed to get away again—and stay away this time. From Fort Thomas, Kentucky, Donald moved to Cincinnati, where in 1975 he found a job as a nursing assistant at the V.A. hospital.

His duties were similar to those he'd performed at Marymount Hospital, so once again, Donald was able to overachieve. Apart from being a nursing aide, he was also a housekeeping assistant. Whenever the patients were not in their rooms—or even when they were, for those who were bedridden—Donald would change linens, clean bathrooms, and do other chores. After a while, he also became a cardiac-catheterization technician and an autopsy assistant.

As an autopsy assistant, Donald had access to the bodies of those who had recently passed. When no one was looking, he would take tissue samples from the bodies for further studies at home. During his ten years at the Cincinnati V.A. hospital, Donald killed more than fifteen people, and no on suspected a thing. His victims included both patients and individuals who posed a threat to him or someone he cared about.

On July 18, 1985, Donald was found in possession of a duffel bag containing suspicious items, including a cocaine spoon, hypodermic needles, surgical scissors and gloves, books on the occult, and a .38 caliber pistol, among others. Upon further investigation, police also found a small specimen of human liver in his locker. But because of errors made during and after the investigation, this particular offense did not result in criminal charges. Instead, Donald was fired and fined $50.00 for bringing a weapon into the hospital.

Donald found himself in between jobs for some time, but was hired as a part-time nursing aide at the Drake Memorial Hospital in 1986. As his previous offense had gone unrecorded, no one questioned his reason for leaving the V.A. hospital. His competence was immediately obvious; he was lauded as an exceptional worker and promoted to a full-time position shortly after he got the job. However, his performance seems to have tapered off thereafter; during an employee evaluation, his evaluator gave him a score of "Good" in six out of ten criteria, and a score of "Acceptable" in the remaining four.

Donald spent a little over a year at the Drake Memorial Hospital. During this time, he committed over 23 murders. Again, some of his victims were patients and the others were people who somehow aggravated him. He had become so confident about killing people that he was no longer scared to do it. He never bothered to hide evidence because he believed that he was untouchable. This proved true until March 7, 1987—the day that John Powell's death was ruled a murder.

Donald Harvey allegedly killed 53 people in the seventeen years that he was working for various healthcare institutions. These institutions have a duty to look after the welfare of their patients, and yet no one noticed anything until Donald went a little overboard with the cyanide. He hid everything in plain sight, yet for seventeen years no one got suspicious. It makes one wonder whether the healthcare system in America is flawed—or if Donald Harvey was just that good.

Personal Life

As Donald jumped through jobs, he had a personal life as well. Involving a number of boyfriends and a flirtation with the occult, it was no less messy than his professional life.

In the early 70s, Donald was healing and recuperating following his rape by Randy White. Color had started returning to a world that had seemed bleak and gray. Donald started to hope, once more, that his life could become better. It was during this time that he met and befriended a man named Vernon Midden, a married undertaker with children.

Despite Vernon's attachments, he and Donald soon became lovers. They were together for seven months. Over the course of their relationship, Vernon taught Donald the secrets of his profession, showing him how bodies would react to actions such as smothering. He also introduced Donald to the occult, but as Donald was not yet a member of his coven, he was not permitted to join the rituals.

In January of 1971, Vernon and Donald's relationship became rocky. They were no longer getting along as well, and fights often ensued. There was no peace to be had while they were together. The fighting kept getting worse, and Donald started becoming depressed. He had also started to fantasize about embalming Vernon alive. Soon after, the fighting escalated, and the relationship died a natural death. While Donald did not harm his ex-lover, he continued to fantasize about it. However, he'd known all along that the relationship was bound to fail, and at least he'd learned some valuable information. Later, when he started his killing spree, he used the information he gleaned from Vernon to hide evidence.

Donald was obviously a disturbed man to have killed as many people as he did, and one facet of that disturbance was a battle with depression. In June of 1971, Donald made his first suicide attempt. Trying to asphyxiate himself, he set fire to the bathroom of an unoccupied unit in his apartment building. The suicide attempt failed when firefighters arrived and saved him, against his wishes. The incident got him jail time and a $50 fine for arson.

After the arson incident, Donald moved to Frankfort, Kentucky, to find a new job. As he did not have much money, he decided to stay with a family that was accepting lodgers. He found himself in the home of Ruth Anne Hodges, a woman about his age, fun and exciting, who made Donald forget about his troubles and taught him how to live.

One day, his host brought him to a party that she was invited to. Between the lights, the drinks, and the dancing, both teens had a good time. When they got back home, giddy and intoxicated, they shed their clothes and headed to the bedroom. While Donald didn't remember exactly what happened—he was very drunk—he did remember being naked with her. This was Donald's first heterosexual experience, as well as how his first child was conceived. Nine months afterward, Ruth Anne gave birth to a healthy baby boy.

Donald then decided to enlist in the Air Force. While he was in basic training, he met a man named Jim and became sexually involved with him. Donald later confessed that he had wanted to kill Jim; he had an inexplicable urge to murder the man he was sleeping with. The only reason he didn't was because he was afraid—not of killing another human being, but of being caught. Jim was well-connected, and Donald knew that there would be a particularly thorough investigation into his death.

Less than a year into his enlistment, Donald became depressed once again. This time he attempted suicide through an overdose of NyQuil. It has been alleged (without evidence) that his superiors then got wind of his confession to killing 15 people at Marymount Hospital. Whether because of that confession, the suicide attempt, or some other reason, he was honorably discharged shortly thereafter. Donald Harvey had no choice but to leave the Air Force.

After his discharge, Donald fell deeper into depression. He struggled with severe mood swings and immense, uncontainable sadness that drove him to unproductiveness and intoxication. Four months after his discharge, Donald was admitted to the V.A. hospital.

He stayed there for a month before being declared normal and released on August 25. Shortly after his release, Donald once again tried to commit suicide. On this occasion his depression was triggered by a family argument. This led him to take huge amounts of Placydil and Equanil in hopes of killing himself. His family rushed him to a hospital, and his stomach was pumped, saving his life. That was apparently as much as they were willing to do for him; they declared him unwelcome in their home shortly afterward.

Following emergency treatment, Donald was readmitted to the V.A. hospital; obviously, the doctors there had been wrong and he was still depressed. He was placed in restraints to keep him from harming himself or others, and over the next month he received 21 electroshock therapy treatments. This time the doctors admitted they hadn't cured his depression, but as he was no longer suicidal, he was released from the hospital on October 17.

Donald then went through a series of jobs in Lexington and Fort Thomas in which he had no access to patients. For three years, from the time that he was released from the V.A. hospital until 1975, Donald Harvey was a good citizen—well, as good as he could get.

Take note that in 1972, Donald Harvey had just turned 20. While many people that age are just on their way to sophomore year, Donald Harvey had already held four jobs, enlisted in the Air Force, and had been admitted to and released from a psych ward. He had also become involved with Russell Addison. They lived together for 10 months, until Donald tired of the relationship and moved on.

After his relationship with Russell, Donald got involved with a man named Ken Estes. They had an intermittent relationship from 1973 to 1978. When they were on good terms, they lived together. When they were not, they lived separately. In the middle of this relationship, 1975, Donald got a job as a nursing assistant at the V.A. hospital in Cincinnati. It was also during this time that he started getting back into an old interest—the occult.

A lot happened over the course of Donald's ten years at the V.A. Once again, he had intimate, unmonitored access to patients, so killing them off and getting away with it was easy. And by 1977, he had finally been admitted to a coven—but not without an initiation. Contrary to Donald's homosexual proclivities, this ceremony required the participation of a heterosexual couple. For this purpose, Donald hooked up with a friend named Jan. During the initiation, Donald and Jan had to switch partners with another couple. This was Donald's second heterosexual encounter, and like the first, it produced a child nine months later. Sometimes, Donald talked about his children fondly, claiming that he loved them both. Other times, when he was going through a rough patch, he would deny any attachment to them—or even their very existence.

After the initiation, Donald received his spirit guide, by the name of Duncan. While he was living, Duncan had been a doctor who attended to those with sicknesses of all kinds. In death, he assisted Donald in picking out his victims.

In 1980, when Donald was 28 years old, he started dating Doug Hill. Like all his other relationships, it was magical in the beginning. Everything was moving smoothly, and Doug was amazing. After a while, though, things once again turned sour. The relationship stood on rocky ground, and the couple started fighting more and more often.

One afternoon, after a particularly heated argument involving many hurtful words, Donald found that he could not control his temper. His pride was wounded, and he would not let that stand. Shortly after the argument, Donald found an opportunity to slip some arsenic into Doug's ice cream. While the arsenic did not kill Doug, it made him severely sick. This was the first time that Donald had attempted to hurt someone outside of a hospital—and it seems to have given him the confidence to do it again.

The ill-fated relationship with Doug lasted only a few months before it ended, but it did not take long for Donald to find a new lover. In August of 1980, Donald moved in with the man who would be his lover for the next six years—Carl Hoeweler. While he did not harm Carl directly until January of 1984, he did harm those he perceived as threats to their relationship.

After he got promoted to Morgue Supervisor at the V.A. Medical Hospital, Donald joined the neo-Nazi National Socialist Party (NSP). Later on, when he was finally caught, he claimed that he was not actually a Nazi sympathizer; he just had friends who were, and he wanted to help them.

In 1983, Donald had a huge fight with Carl's parents. Donald was both annoyed at Carl for not siding with him and angry at his parents for starting the fight. Within a few months, Donald had killed Carl's father and made numerous attempts to kill his mother. Even though Carl did not know that his partner was harming his family, he made Donald move out of their house in January of 1984. Their relationship continued until 1986, but because he felt rejected, Donald attempted to kill Carl many times in those two years. He was unsuccessful.

In 1986, after Donald had killed and harmed a great many people, his trust in Carl started to wane. He was convinced that Carl was on to him and would soon turn him in. This distrust naturally took a major toll on their relationship. They started fighting more often and throwing nasty words at each other. Finally, in mid-year, they broke up.

After the breakup, Donald started seeing Dr. Mark Barbara, a psychiatrist. He made another suicide attempt the same month. He was drowning in depression once more, and one day he could no longer take it. He got his car keys, started the engine, and just drove. On a deserted mountain road, he decided that he could no longer take the utter sorrow that was consuming him. In one swift turn of the steering wheel, Donald Harvey drove straight off a cliff. He received a head injury, but survived.

To cope with his depression, he started delving more deeply into the occult. He found some solace in joining occult activities and performing their rituals.

His killing spree continued, too, and over a year, he was able to kill 23 to 26 people—reports vary. With one of his victims, though, he got careless. Donald made a mistake in killing a man named John Powell, and the body was autopsied by a forensic psychologist, Dr. Lee Lehman. While no one knows how he slipped up, Donald was arrested, tried, and convicted shortly thereafter. He spent the remainder of his life in prison.

The First Kill

Donald committed his first murder on May 30, 1970. It was a night like any other. He was working late at Marymount Hospital. A stroke victim by the name of Logan Evans had just been admitted, and Donald was the assigned orderly. As he entered the room to check on the eighty-eight-year-old man, he noticed that he was no longer functioning normally.

As he got closer to the patient to clean him up and check on his vital signs, Logan decided to wipe feces on his face. For Donald, this was not just an affront to his person, but also to his pride—and it was also the last straw. Donald had just gone into the room to help the old man—and he returned that kindness by smearing feces on his face.

This indignity pushed Donald over the edge. Enraged, he grabbed a pillow and a piece of blue plastic and stuffed it over the old man's face. He held it there until he was sure he could not breathe. The plastic barrier was to ensure that no feather particles would be found in his victim's airways, and to make sure that Logan was truly dead, Donald used a stethoscope to monitor his heartbeat. These facts showcase the terrifyingly brilliant nature of Donald Harvey: Even in a state of overwhelming anger, he was still able to think clearly.

Only after his victim was dead did he realize what he had done. This act of anger had broken something inside—the barrier between right and wrong suddenly became hazy. This first kill did not scare him; rather, it empowered him. He'd been someone who had absolutely no choices in life. Suddenly, he called the shots. He could decide who would live and who would die. This first kill was important because it defined his life thereafter.

The surprising thing was that Donald was not scared. After killing Logan, he cleaned him up like nothing had happened. He cleaned himself up, as well. After he was sure that the room looked normal, he disposed of the plastic bag and alerted the nurse on duty. He strutted about as if he had done nothing wrong, had not just killed a living human being because he'd gotten mad. Donald was not afraid of getting caught. Neither the nurse nor the doctors found anything suspicious about the death of Logan Evans, and the body was disposed of without an autopsy.

After this kill, Donald began a killing spree, murdering a number of patients at Marymount Hospital. He stopped killing from the time he entered the Air Force until he became a nursing assistant at the V.A. hospital. He claimed that he was able to control his urges during those years, but most psychologists believe that there were just fewer opportunities.

This first kill changed many things for Donald. From a powerless man, he became a god. To the world, he became a murderer. To himself, he became free.

The Serial Killer

After committing his first murder, Donald felt that he could wrap the world around his little finger and make everyone in it do his bidding. As he was a manipulative person by nature, no one suspected that he was capable of doing the heinous things that he did. He even confessed a number of times, but was still not caught.

In a number of interviews, Donald confessed to feeling empowered and in control when he killed—which was why he loved doing it. He had been a child who had no control over his own fate, who was restricted by both circumstances and people. Now he decided whether someone would live or die. He perfected the art of using cyanide and arsenic in small, lethal, undetectable doses so that his killing would go unnoticed—and for the most part, it did.

Donald Harvey was not born a serial killer. The world made him that way. Fate dealt him an ugly hand, and he decided what to do with his cards. If he had not become so confident and arrogant, he might have gotten away with even more than the 57 officially recognized murders or the 87 that he claimed. While Harvey was lethal, society was harsh to him, as well. It was no wonder that he became a serial killer.

The Victims

After his first kill, Donald Harvey committed many more. He admitted to 87 murders, but was only convicted of 36 because evidence for the rest could not be found. In 1987, when Donald pleaded guilty to avoid the death penalty, he was made to confess to all of his crimes. A stipulation in his sentence was that he had to recount the details of all his murders for an official record. If he complied, he would avoid the electric chair—and he did. Here is the complete account of all of his victims—the ones he remembered, at least.

As already recounted, his first victim was Logan Evans, an 88-year-old stroke victim.

His second victim was a man named James Tyree, a sixty-nine year old patient at Marymount Hospital. Donald did not kill James intentionally. Rather, he accidentally inserted the wrong-sized catheter. James did not protest at first, but after he started to feel the pain, he cried out for Donald to remove the catheter. In his panic, he held the old man down until he started vomiting blood and eventually died.

Donald's third victim was his first female victim, as well as his first kill as the Angel of Death. Donald had heard Elizabeth Wyatt praying for death, and she had even explicitly told him that she wanted to die. So one night, as she slept soundly, he turned her oxygen supply to a very low level. Four hours later, a nurse found her dead. No one suspected a thing. Elizabeth was 44 when she died.

At age 43, Eugene McQueen was already a long-time patient at Marymount. Doctors advised everyone who attended to McQueen that he was not to be turned on his stomach, as it would be dangerous to his health. Donald, of course, turned him over anyway, and Eugene died by drowning in his own fluids. Donald immediately notified the nurse that the patient looked bad, but she told him that nothing was wrong. To avoid suspicion, Donald bathed the body and placed it back in the room. This incident was covered up by the hospital, as it was a failure of the nurse on duty to recognize that her patient had died, but Donald's coworkers remembered it for another reason: They teased him about bathing a dead man for the entire duration of his stay at Marymount.

Sometime after this incident, Donald accidentally used a faulty gas tank on a patient named Harvey Williams, who died at the age of 82 from cardiac arrest. After Harvey's death, Donald hid the tank away, thinking that it might come in useful someday.

Donald next committed his first premeditated murder. One of his patients, Ben Gilbert, had hit him on the head with a urinal so hard that Donald passed out. Ben, who was mentally deranged and thought that Donald was a burglar, had then poured the urine all over his unconscious victim. Perhaps reminded of the feces-smearing incident with Logan Evans, Donald lost his temper and got very angry at Ben.

One day, after careful planning, Donald entered Ben's room with a coat hanger. Ben, in his impaired state of mind, did not find this strange. After making sure that the room was secure, Donald changed out Ben's size #18 catheter with a female-sized #20 catheter. This put Ben in tremendous pain, but Donald was not done yet. He straightened out the coat hanger and shoved it into the catheter. Ben went into a coma from the shock. The hanger had punctured his bladder and bowel.

After Ben was unconscious, Harvey cleaned him and the room and made sure that nothing looked amiss. He reinserted the correct catheter and disposed of the female one and the hanger. Four days later, Ben passed away.

On August 15, 1970, Donald found a use for the broken gas tank he'd hidden. A woman named Maude Nichols was admitted to Marymount with horrible bedsores. The bedsores were so bad that maggots were crawling in most of them. Neither Donald nor anyone else wanted to deal with that, so he put the poor woman out of her misery by using the faulty gas tank to hasten her death.

Fifteen days after killing Maude, he killed a man name William Bowling. The 58-year-old man had been admitted because he had difficulty in breathing, and Donald killed him by failing to turn on his oxygen tank. This was among Donald's mercy kills, as he saw that the old man was suffering from his ailment. William died of a massive heart attack shortly afterward.

Donald then proceeded to kill four more victims using the faulty gas tank. The first was a woman named Viola Reed Wyan. She was a 63-year-old who suffered from leukemia and electrolyte imbalance. After trying unsuccessfully to end her suffering by smothering her, Donald retrieved the gas tank from its hiding place. After her, Donald killed an 80-year-old man named Sam Carroll. Donald felt that the man had suffered enough from his ailments—pneumonia and a blockage in his small intestine—so he prematurely ended his life. He then murdered Silas Butner, age 62, to end his suffering from kidney problems. Next came John V. Combs, an 82-year-old with heart and respiratory problems. Again, Donald had initially tried to suffocate him, but after a number of failed attempts, he brought out his trusty gas tank.

Those four murders were committed with the notion of ending suffering, but that does not seem to have been the motive for Donald's last three murders at Marymount Hospital. He killed a 91-year-old woman named Margaret Harrison by giving her an overdose of Demerol, morphine, and codeine. (This may have been an accident, as the drugs he administered were actually meant for another patient.)

His next victim was a woman named Maggie Rawlins. She was admitted to Marymount for a severe burn on her left arm. Unfortunately for her, Donald made her his next target. He killed her the same way he killed his first victim, by smothering her until he was sure that she was no longer breathing.

After Maggie, Donald claimed the life of his last victim at Marymount Hospital: Milton Bryant Sasser. He killed the 90-year-old man by administering an overdose of morphine, but here he made a mistake. The problem was that he tried to dispose of the needle by flushing it down the toilet. The drain clogged and the needle was discovered. However, no one suspected that there was a serial killer in their midst, much less that it was Donald. Even when he quit after the incident, he was not linked to any deaths at the hospital.

On record, Donald killed fifteen people at Marymount Hospital in the span of 10 months. He chose his victims randomly. While he liked to think that he was an Angel of Death, his kills at Marymount disproved that conceit. It is true that he chose some of his victims because they were suffering immensely, but others he killed for no reason other than his own sick desire for control. It is harrowing to think that Donald was only 18 at the time that he committed these crimes.

For five years after killing Milton Bryant Sasser, Donald was a relatively normal citizen. While he was incarcerated once before enlisting in the Air Force, for arson during a suicide attempt, he did not kill anyone. He went through bouts of depression and even entered a mental facility, but he left the Air Force with an honorable discharge.

And then Donald found a job at the Cincinnati V.A. hospital as a nursing assistant—and there, once again, he started killing his patients.

His first victim after his 5-year break was a man named Joseph Harris. Going back to his old tricks, Donald killed Joseph by tampering with his oxygen tank to reduce the flow.

When Joseph succumbed, Donald remembered the rush he felt whenever he killed someone—whenever he played God. Suddenly, he remembered the intoxicating feeling of ultimate control. He fell of the wagon, and he fell hard.

Donald confessed to killing another four men after Joseph—but he could not remember how he killed them. Their names were James Twitty, James Ritter, Harry Rhodes, and Sterling Moore. All four died in his ward, but none of their deaths were linked to the new nursing assistant.

After having killed 20 people, Donald was confident in himself and in his abilities to evade suspicion. This confidence led him to harm his first victim outside of a hospital. As a nursing assistant, Donald had access to chemicals not available to most people. Slowly, he began to amass large quantities of the cyanide and arsenic with which he would kill his victims.

His first target outside the hospital was his lover Doug Hill, with whom he'd had an argument. As described above, Donald slipped some arsenic into Doug's ice cream. Doug did not die, but he got very sick.

His next victim was his lover of six years, Carl Hoeweler. Donald found out that Carl was warming the beds of other men every Monday. Determined to make sure that his lover could not cheat on him, Donald took to slipping arsenic into Carl's Sunday dinners—just enough to make him too ill to go out the next day.

Donald's attempts at harming others became worse and worse. His next victim was Carl's best female friend, a woman named Diane Alexander. Donald thought that Diane was a threat to his and Carl's relationship. He referred to her unflatteringly as his lover's "fag hag." As time passed, and she showed no signs of leaving Carl alone, Donald found that he wanted to hurt her. He started planning his next harmful act—and it would be worse than ever. This was not going to be a regular murder; he wanted to hurt her—and bad.

One night, he snuck some Hepatitis B serum out of the hospital. The next time he had access to Diane's drink, he stealthily poured in the serum, watching with a sense of triumph as she drank it down. Diane became infected with the virus, and emboldened by his success, Donald also tried to infect her with HIV. Luckily, he was unsuccessful in this second attempt.

This success sated Donald's urge to harm others for three years. It seemed that his killing spree was over—until he set his eyes on his neighbor, Helen Metzger. He thought that the 64-year-old woman was a danger to both him and Carl. He never explained exactly what threat he thought the old woman posed, but for whatever reason he developed a plan to harm—and eventually kill—her.

First, he sprinkled arsenic on some leftovers and mixed it into a jar of mayonnaise. Posing as a good neighbor, he shared these with Helen. Several weeks later, he gave her an arsenic-contaminated pie. After ingesting a significant amount of arsenic, Metzger developed paralysis. Shortly after that, she started hemorrhaging, and she passed away later the same week. According to the official report, Metzger died of Guillaine-Barre Syndrome, a muscle weakness brought about by a deteriorating immune system that damages the nerves.

Helen was mourned by her family, but no one even suspected that her neighbor had killed her. When they went to clean up the deceased woman's belongings, her family partook of some of the mayonnaise that Donald had given her. They all got sick shortly thereafter, but assumed it was just food poisoning. After all, no one ever suspects that they have ingested arsenic! Fortunately, no one else died.

After Helen's death, Carl's parents decided to come over and check in on their son. They fought with Donald continuously during the visit. After one heated argument too many, Donald got fed up with it all. He decided it was time for Mr. and Mrs. Hoeweler to say goodbye—permanently.

Dipping into his stash of arsenic, he started to give Carl's parents a little every day in their food. He knew that he wouldn't have to wait long for the poison to take effect. On May 1, 1983, after five days of ingesting arsenic, Henry Hoeweler suffered a sudden stroke. He was rushed to the hospital and saved. Unfortunately for him, the Angel of Death visited his room and snuck some additional arsenic into his pudding. This last dose of the poison was the end of Mr. Hoeweler. He died in his sleep. The official report said that the cause of death was kidney failure.

For the following year, Donald continued to poison Carl's mother. While she did not die, she suffered from various ailments.

During this time, Donald was amassing a collection of arsenic and cyanide. He didn't want anyone to discover this, of course, so he would remove the labels off his stolen bottles. To do this, he used wood alcohol, scientifically known as methyl alcohol or methanol. It is a powerful solvent—and a deadly poison. Unfortunately for Carl's brother-in-law, Howard Vetter, Donald kept his wood alcohol in a vodka bottle. Carl served some of this "vodka" to Howard, and after a week of being sick, he suffered a heart attack and died of cardiac arrest.

Donald's second accidental victim was a patient named Hiram Proffit, who died when Donald inadvertently gave him the wrong dosage of heparin. He didn't report his error, and no one found out about the mishap.

After two accidental killings, Donald committed another deliberate one. He murdered the first boyfriend he'd ever had, James Peluso, because the man asked him for sexual favors when he could no longer take care of himself. Donald was insulted by this callous request and set out to kill his former lover. One day, while they were having a meal, Donald slipped some arsenic into James's daiquiri and pudding. James died shortly after being admitted to the V.A. hospital. No one questioned the 65-year-old man's death because he had already been having cardiac problems.

Donald then proceeded to kill a neighbor named Edward Wilson. Edward believed that Carl was cheating him on his utility bills, and Donald was afraid that he would take legal action. He snuck some arsenic into the older man's Pepto-Bismol, and five days later he was declared dead.

On record, Donald killed 11 people during his stay at the Cincinnati V.A. hospital. Six of them were patients; the rest were accidents or people he deemed threats to himself or Carl. He harmed four individuals and an entire family by infecting them with viruses or poisoning them with arsenic. Among his victims were Carl Hoeweler's parents—and even Carl himself. Donald could not control his urge to harm and kill. The power went to his head, and he did not want to stop.

Donald was finally fired from the V.A. hospital after he was found in possession of a duffel bag full of suspicious items. Because this incident did not go on his record, he was able to get a job at Daniel Drake Memorial in Cincinnati shortly after. This would be the last job that Donald would ever have.

Just six weeks after he was hired, the Angel of Death struck again. With the help of his spirit guide, Duncan, he chose his next victim. Duncan pointed to a man named Nathani J. Watson, a semi-comatose 65-year-old. Nathani was being fed through a gastric tube, and was clearly suffering. Donald felt that no man should live that way, so he did what he thought he had to.

He repeatedly attempted to kill Nathani with a wet plastic garbage can liner, but he was always interrupted. He finally succeeded in killing him by pushing the liner into his mouth and nostrils, then cleaned up the scene like nothing had happened. A nurse found Nathani's dead body in the ward 45 minutes later. No investigation was conducted. Donald later rationalized this murder by saying that Nathani was a rapist anyway, although this was never proven.

Nathani's death started a killing spree that Donald reveled in. Four days later, he killed a 64-year-old man named Leon Nelson in the same way, by smothering him with a wet plastic garbage can liner. The next week, Donald put rat poison into Virgil

Weedle's food. At 81 years old, Virgil died of a heart attack. Donald took some cookies left by his family to perform a ceremony with Duncan.

The next day, he moved on to his next victim and attempted to kill Lawrence Berndsen with rat poison. Lawrence was transferred to a nursing home on the same day and died three days later. Twelve days afterward, on May 2nd, Carl broke up with Donald, and Donald fell into depression. On the very night of the breakup, Donald put cyanide in Doris Nally's apple juice. No one knows why he did it, on orders from Duncan or because of his depression or both, but Doris died before the night was over.

Donald also attempted to murder Willie Johnson. He slipped arsenic into Johnson's food four times, but was unsuccessful in putting the man to rest. In a little over a month, Donald killed Edward Schreibeis by seasoning his soup with arsenic. No autopsy was conducted on the 63-year-old man. A week after that, Donald killed 80-year-old Robert Crockett. The old man was hooked up to an I.V., and Donald saw the opportunity to poison him with cyanide injected through the tube. Another week later, Donald injected cyanide directly into Donald Barney's buttocks. To make sure that he died, Donald also gave the 61-year-old man cyanide through his feeding tube.

The next fortnight passed peacefully, but then Donald slipped a cyanide solution into James T. Woods's gastric tube. The old man died on July 25, and again no autopsy was conducted. Three weeks later, Donald put a cyanide solution in Ernst C. Fray's gastric tube. He was becoming more and more confident. No autopsies were ever conducted on his victims, and no one suspected a thing. Emboldened, he even stole a pair of boots belonging to Ernst. Then he struck again with cyanide, putting the poisonous chemical solution in Milton Canter's nasal tube.

Donald had apparently decided he liked taking things from his victims; from Milton he took a blanket.

He killed his next seven victims in a similar manner, sneaking cyanide solution into their tubes or dissolving it in their beverages. A little less than three weeks after Milton's death, on September 17, 1986, Donald snuck cyanide into Roger Evan's gastric tube. Three days later, he did the same thing to Clayborn Kendrick, while also injecting the cyanide solution into the 69-year-old's testes. In a little over a month, he made Albert Buehlmann drink water laced with dissolved cyanide. The next day, he killed William Collins by making him ingest cyanide-spiked orange juice.

Donald took a five-day break and then resumed his killing spree. He mixed cyanide in water and administered it to Henry Cody through his gastric tube. The man died at 78 years old on November 4th. Two weeks later, he did the same thing to Mose Thompson. In a few hours, Thompson passed away as well. In another two weeks, Donald took the life of Odas Day with a cyanide solution. And the next day, he gave Cleo Fish a cranberry-juice-and-cyanide cocktail. After her death, Donald took a lock of her hair to use in performing a ritual with Duncan.

In the span of five months, Donald had killed seven people without remorse. His confidence levels were reaching an all-time high because no one suspected a thing. In six out of the seven cases, autopsies were either not performed or not permitted. Upon Milton Canter's death, the doctors requested an autopsy, but were denied by the man's family because of Jewish restrictions. Upon Roger Evans's death, an autopsy was performed, but no cyanide was found. Donald felt that he had become untouchable, invincible—a god.

Before the year ended, Donald attempted to murder two more victims with arsenic: Harold White and John Oldendick. Luckily for them, he miscalculated and gave them doses that were too small to be fatal. During his confession, Donald said he believed that John was actually healed by this attempt on his life.

Ten days into the new year, Donald killed Leo Parker by giving him cyanide through his feed bag. Again, an autopsy was conducted, and again, no poison was found. He felt unstoppable. No one was going to catch him. He had mastered the art of killing his victims without leaving a trace.

The next month, he poisoned Margaret Kuckro and Stella Lemon by dissolving cyanide into their orange juice. While Margaret died shortly after the poisoning, it took several weeks for Stella to succumb.

After these two kills, Donald switched to a new murder weapon, choosing to poison his next two victims with Detachol, an adhesive remover. On March 6, he slipped some Detachol into Joseph Pike's food, killing him instantly. The next day, he fed the adhesive remover to Hilda Leitz dissolved in her orange juice. Both patients died, and no autopsies were performed.

On the same day he killed Hilda, Donald also poisoned his last victim, John Powell. John had spent months in a coma after a motorcycle accident, but he was starting to improve. Doctors and nurses were therefore surprised when he suddenly died. They had expected him to recover, and his sudden death baffled them. An autopsy was performed—and as fate had it, the assistant coroner was a biochemist who was very familiar with both cyanide and arsenic.

On March 8, 1987, Dr. Lee Lehman opened up John Powell's body and smelled the scent of bitter almonds wafting from the dead man's organs. He immediately identified the cyanide and sent the report and some samples to three labs for testing and confirmation. The labs verified that there was indeed cyanide in Powell's remains. He had not died from natural causes.

Everyone was a suspect. Donald was in trouble for the first time.

The Investigation and Guilty Plea

When Dr. Lehman smelled the bitter almond scent on John Powell's body, he immediately knew that there was something wrong—specifically, that someone had murdered John with cyanide. He wanted to be sure, though, so he sent out tissue samples to three different laboratories to either confirm or deny his suspicions.

Within the month, the laboratories sent back their reports, confirming that there was cyanide in the samples. Someone had poisoned John Powell. The police were alerted immediately. There was a killer in the hospital, and they needed to find him before more people were killed. No time was wasted, and in the ensuing investigation, all of the hospital staff members were suspects.

The police started questioning each individual who had come into contact with John—his widow, his family members, his friends. They were thorough with their investigation. As the cyanide had been ingested, they needed to know what John's last meal was, whom he ate it with, and who had prepared it.

They also needed to know who had been in regular contact with John and whether he had any enemies. Looking at the evidence, the authorities concluded that the killer must be a member of the hospital staff. No one could have had access to both John's food and a stash of cyanide unless they were working at the hospital. John's widow, family members, and friends were ruled out as suspects.

So the police began interviewing the hospital staff one by one. In one of the interviews, someone brought up Donald's troubled past, describing how he had left his previous employers for reasons unknown—and in a hurry, to top that. Another interview revealed that many of his coworkers at Drake Memorial had taken to calling Donald the Angel of Death—not because they suspected his crimes, but because he was so often present when a patient passed away.

With this information in hand, the police started to focus their suspicions on Donald. And since the hospital employees had volunteered to take polygraph tests, the police decided it was time to accept the offer. When Donald got wind of this, he felt despair. For the first time in seventeen years, it looked like he was about to get caught. He could not escape the polygraph test.

But this did not stop Donald from trying. Even though he had attempted suicide multiple times, he now suddenly realized that he did not truly want to die. He bought a book that promised to teach him how to beat a polygraph, but without being able to test what he had learned, he knew that success was hardly guaranteed. Contrary to his usual confident and cool persona, Donald Harvey was starting to get nervous.

His nerves just got worse as the date of the polygraph test neared. When the date finally arrived and he still wasn't sure he could beat it, he bailed. He decided to call in sick and skip the polygraph test altogether.

We will never know what Donald was thinking and feeling during this time, but his failure to show up on the testing date naturally raised the suspicions of the police. They assigned two more detectives to the case, Jim Lawson and Ron Camden, and these men brought Donald in for questioning.

Donald did not confess right away. He did not want to get sent to jail, or worse, death row. He held his tongue and did not budge as the detectives interrogated him. But they kept trying different techniques to wear him down, and slowly, his resolve melted.

After a few grueling hours of "good cop, bad cop," Donald confessed—albeit it was a half-baked confession.

Donald said that he'd felt sorry for John Powell. He was comatose, and Donald saw how his family mourned him even while he was still alive. He saw their pain at being so close to their loved one and yet still so far. He confessed that he had decided that no man should live like that and put cyanide in his gastric tube to end his misery.

Donald also stated that he had killed no one else. He told the detectives that John was an isolated case and that it was a mercy killing. The two were not convinced. They obtained a search warrant and headed over to Donald's home in Middletown.

The detectives were astounded at what they found in the apartment. They found 30 pounds of cyanide that Donald had amassed over the years, enough to poison a small town. They also found jars of arsenic, books on the occult, materials for performing rituals, other poisons, and even Donald's diary. The evidence strongly suggested that their suspicions were correct—John was not an isolated case.

On April 6, 1987, Donald Harvey was charged with one count of aggravated murder and finally arrested. Hoping to escape jail time, Donald entered a plea of not guilty by reason of insanity, as recorded by his public defender, William Whalen. The prosecutor allowed this, but the judge ordered that Donald be held on a $200,000 bond until the hearings were over.

A month later, Dr. Schmidtgoessling and clinical psychologist Roger Fisher conducted a competency hearing. They concluded that Donald was depressed, but sane. He could not plead insanity because he could tell right from wrong and the hearing had proved that he was not psychotic.

The media had a field day with the story. People were interested in this new case that starred a mercy killer known as the Angel of Death—it even went on the front page of the *Cincinnati Enquirer*. While most of the news outlets merely reported the current charges (i.e. Donald Harvey was a mercy killer who had killed only one victim, John Powell), a news anchor at WCPO-TV sensed that there was more to the story.

The anchor, Pat Minarcin, asked one of his reporters if the police were further investigating the case and looking into the possibility of Donald being a serial killer. When the reporter answered no, Pat knew that he had to conduct his own investigation.

While he did not question the police on air, he did start looking into the case. Four days after his report, he received an anonymous call from Drake Memorial Hospital. The woman did not disclose her name, but she did provide Pat with a list of potential victims of Donald. She said that there was something suspicious going on, but her superiors were turning a blind eye.

The next day, the woman called again, this time with two other nurses who were able to provide three more names. The three women reported that they had told their supervisor about their suspicions, but she had done nothing. At first, she denied the possibility that Donald Harvey was a serial killer. Later, she told the three women to keep quiet about their suspicions. Because of this, they were unwilling to disclose their identities, but they promised to keep in touch. They could, however, provide no evidence to substantiate their claims.

Because Pat did not want to discourage the women, he could not openly investigate the case for fear of spooking or aggravating their superiors at the hospital. He got copies of the death certificates of the sixteen people on his list, but this proved useless: they were all reported to have died of natural causes. Donald had made sure of that.

Just as Pat thought he was at a dead end, the women called again. By this point, the anchor was annoyed somewhat annoyed with these women; they could not give him enough evidence, and they did not want to give him their names. To move things forward, he proposed to meet them even though he was supposed to go on air in 20 minutes. He told the news director that he was on the verge of a huge story and that he needed to skip the news report for the day.

The director hesitantly allowed him to go, and Pat met with the women. There were now five of them. They told him their story and gave him a longer list people that Donald might have killed—a total of 33 people. Pat found out that the nurses' caution stemmed from a recent meeting with their superiors. The hospital heads had informed the staff that an internal investigation showed that John Powell was an isolated case. The superiors also told the staff that the police had confirmed their findings and that they should not talk to the press.

These five women could lose their jobs by talking to him. They were going against the hospital administrators' explicit orders. Pat knew that the hospital was hiding something. It was just a matter of time before he figured it out.

Pat obtained the death certificates of all 33 people on the list. While the hospital had gotten wind of his investigation, he did not stop. The hospital branded him as an opportunist who was spreading false rumors in hopes of attracting viewers. This did not discourage Pat in the slightest. Rather, it made him even more convinced that the hospital was hiding something.

While he knew that something was wrong, Pat could not find the link. He could not find proof that Donald had killed those 33 people—until he looked into Donald's work schedule. One day, while all the papers were laid out on his desk, arranged by date and time of death, Pat decided to compare his findings with Donald's work schedule. He got a hit. A pattern emerged that showed a close link between Donald and the deaths of the people on his list. There was now no denying that Donald had killed the 33—but could Pat report this?

While he had solid—if circumstantial—evidence, he could not air the story without the risk of angering the hospital and being sued. So he contacted Donald's public defender, William Whalen, with the story. While the lawyer was irritated at the suggestion that John Powell hadn't been Donald's only victim—which directly contradicted the hospital and police report—the thought kept him up at night.

Finally, William decided to ask Donald directly: Had he killed anyone else? Unhesitatingly, Donald gave him a small nod. Suddenly, what had seemed like an easy case became much more difficult, and William was faced with a dilemma. From an Angel of Death, Donald had become a serial killer.

When William asked him for a number, Donald said that he could not answer that question because he did not know the exact figure. When Donald told him that he thought he had killed around 70 people, William was distraught. He had expected that Donald might have killed two or three more people, but not 70. He did not know what to do, but he realized that a plea of insanity would not work.

He needed to find some leverage with which to bargain for Harvey's life. After two weeks, William phoned Pat and told him to air the story. Pat was surprised that the lawyer would throw the case; he did not realize that his report would allow Donald to keep his life.

After the report was aired, the Cincinnati media went into a frenzy. Was Donald Harvey a serial killer? Had the official investigations been inadequate? Was the hospital covering up for their mistakes?

Suddenly, the case had burst wide open and no one was sure of anything. Pat even obtained a copy of the interrogation tape, which showed that Donald did not answer the question of whether he had killed other people. The report showed that Donald was more than just a mercy killer. He was a serial killer, and someone needed to look into it.

The Confession and Sentence

Evidence was piling up against Donald, and he could no longer hide behind a claim of insanity. William decided to draft a plea bargain. As the news reports were pressuring the justice system to get the facts straight, prosecutor Art Ney was willing to hear him out.

The suspicion that this was not an isolated case—that the police had a serial killer in custody—was growing. The general public needed to know that they were safe, and the prosecutor needed to know the truth to seek a just sentence.

So when William stepped forward with the plea bargain, the prosecutor accepted it. The terms were that Donald would recount all of his murders and explain them in detail. In exchange, Donald would escape the electric chair and get jail time instead.

On August 18, 1987, Donald Harvey pled guilty to one count of felonious assault, four counts of attempted murder, and 25 counts of aggravated murder. Succeeding confessions raised the aggravated murder count to 36. He was handed three 20-years-to-life sentences and fined $270,000.

In 1988, he went before the Hamilton County Pleas Court, where he was indicted for three more murders and three more attempted murders. For each of the murders, he was sentenced to 20 years to life. For each of the attempted murders, he was sentenced to 10 to 25 years. These sentences would run concurrently with his previous sentences.

On September 6, 1988, Donald agreed to confess to all of his murders at Marymount Hospital on tape. While he confessed to thirteen killings, he was only convicted of nine, as four of them could not be confirmed. He was charged with eight counts of murder and one count of voluntary manslaughter. Ohio Circuit Judge Lewis Hopper sentenced him to life imprisonment for each of the murders and 20 years for the count of manslaughter. Again, these sentences would run concurrently with his sentences in Hamilton County.

After Donald received multiple life sentences, $235,000,000 worth of lawsuits were filed against him in Hamilton County. Jan Taylor, Donald's superior at the Drake Memorial Hospital, pled guilty to one count of falsifying public documents, but faced no jail time.

The revelations also brought changes to all three hospitals that Donald had worked in. According to the Cincinnati Magazine, the Drake Memorial Hospital became "an independent, nonprofit, rehabilitation and long-term care facility affiliated with the University of Cincinnati College of Medicine."

Over 17 years, Donald Harvey killed 87 people—and he almost got away with it. But justice did catch up with him, and he was set for parole in 2047 at the earliest.

The Final End

Donald Harvey was a convicted murderer—a serial killer, in fact—but he was charming, handsome, and cunning. No one who came into contact with him knew the demons that lurked beneath his skin. Even his appointed public defender, William Whalen, did not doubt his first confession until news anchor Pat Minarcin started his investigation. The man known as the Angel of Death was smart and manipulative, and he repaid the Fates for the bad cards they had dealt him by ending the lives of others.

Finally, someone ended his. On March 30, 2017, Donald Harvey took his final breath. The incarcerated serial killer had been found beaten to a pulp in his cell in the state prison at Toledo two days before. After two decades of killing innocents, and three more in prison, Donald Harvey had finally met his end.

For more than half of his life, Donald Harvey was an inmate at the Toledo Correctional Institute. He was punished for the crimes that he had committed from the time he was just 18 years old. If he had lived for another 26 years, he would have been eligible for parole at the age of 91.

According to his testimony, he had started killing because he wanted to ease the pain of suffering patients. Later on, he killed those he thought might harm him. Ultimately, the Angel of Death, as he liked to be called, became a murderer. While he was definitely disturbed, and his childhood was horrifying, nothing could excuse the crimes he committed.

Testimonials

The end of 1988 was also the end of investigations surrounding Donald's murder victims. The investigative team gave up on account of the lack of substantial evidence to convict the man of any more murders.

Throughout his 35th year, Donald was herded from one courtroom to another, charged with the murder of more and more people. By the end the year, even though prosecutors could not convict him for all of his murders, he had 28 concurrent sentences.

Various people were interviewed about their opinions on Donald. After all that he had done, only his mother still thought him a good boy. The charming and friendly Donald was no more. People saw his true colors and were astounded at his manipulation and crimes.

But even after he was convicted and imprisoned, his mother still loved him dearly. The National Post reports that she still claimed he was a "good boy." She said that he was just sick, and that he just needed medical attention. She also alleged that he had been released too early from the psych ward in 1972, and that the doctors there were to blame for her son's continuing mental illness.

Prosecuting Attorney Joe Detters, on the other hand, said that Donald had gotten what he deserved. The man had committed cold-blooded murder and still had the gall to claim the name Angel of Death, suggesting that he killed for mercy. Attorney Detters repeatedly said that if Donald was ever released from prison, he would start killing again. The world would never be safe, so long as this man was in it.

Another prosecutor recounted that Donald was not even a bit remorseful. During the trial, when the prosecution brought out a 4-foot-by-8-foot board containing all the names of his victims, Donald chuckled. He believed that he did those people favors by ending their lives. Until his final breath, he believed that he'd done no wrong.

The same prosecutor said that Donald got the nickname "Kiss of Death" because after each of his kills, he would joke about it by saying, "I got another one today." His coworkers never suspected that there was truth behind his words.

Another prosecutor called Harvey out for claiming the name Angel of Death. Robert Hamel, a former judge, said that Donald knew what he was doing—that he decided that "he had the right to decide who lives and who dies, and it was wrong." Hamel claimed that, contrary to his projected image, Donald was completely sane and he knew he was doing wrong by murdering people.

His lawyer, William Whalen, on the other hand, said that it was not hard to like the man. Donald was intelligent and soft-spoken. When questioned about the murder of Powell, he had confidently answered that it was an isolated case, and that he had never killed anyone before that.

William truly thought that Donald had good intentions—until evidence proved otherwise. When he learned that Donald was a serial killer instead of a one-time mercy killer, William did not know how to defend him. He even went to his church to seek advice on how to handle the situation—how to defend a man knowing that he had done horrible things.

When he met Donald, William thought that he was a man with good intentions who had done something horrible as a result. By the end of the affair, even William could not truly defend his client with a clear conscience.

Lastly, Kathy Young, daughter of Clayborn Kendrick, recounted tales from Donald's diary. She said that it contained a detailed account of how he murdered each of his victims. Donald truly thought that he was doing his victims favors. In the case of Clayborn, Kathy recounted that Donald had waited for her mother to leave for Hawaii before killing her father. Donald had rescheduled the murder to accommodate Mrs. Kendrick's vacation.

Even while he was committing horrific crimes, he was charming. He had a boyish gait, and he always took care of his appearance. Everyone who knew him said that he was a regular man—smarter than most, but normal.

In 1991, Donald gave an interview to the Columbus Dispatch. He said that he got away with most of his crimes because the doctors were overworked. They would not check on the bodies themselves; instead, they sent residents or trainees to pronounce the patient dead and send them directly to the funeral homes.

Donald also said that he believed that he was doing the world favors by killing people. He claimed to have been "putting people out of their misery," and even went so far as to say that he wished someone would do the same for him if he ever got sick enough.

When asked again why he did such things, Donald answered that he liked the feeling of control. Other people had controlled and abused him since he was a small boy. Suddenly having the power to make the ultimate choice of life and death was intoxicating to a man who'd had no power before that. In another interview, Donald said, "You think I played God, and I did." (William Whalen retorted by saying, "[He did it] because he could. He knew how to do it.")

Though different people have different opinions surrounding Donald's state of mind, one thing is for sure: He killed dozens of people, and no one suspected him. While he battled with depression, he was still sane. He fooled himself into thinking that he was doing the right thing.

The Death of the Angel and Similar Cases

Donald Harvey died on March 30, 2017. Two days before, prison guards had found him severely beaten in his prison cell at the Toledo Correctional Institute. According to the police report, an unarmed person entered Donald's cell on March 28, 2017, and attacked him. He was found in critical condition and died two days later. While police are looking into the crime, the case isn't a priority. Donald was a serial killer, and many believe that he got what he deserved.

Donald Harvey was 64 years old when he died, 30 years before he would have been eligible for parole. In a news report, a relative of one of his victims stated that she was not happy about his death. Donald had done the damage, and even if he was gone from the world, his passing did not bring back her loved one.

The sad thing is that while Donald Harvey was possibly the most prolific hospital serial killer, he was not the only one. There are others who did what he did—killed the helpless while they were supposed to be providing healthcare.

On February 21, 1991, a British nurse named Beverly Allitt killed her first victim, a 7-month-old boy named Liam Taylor. The infant was admitted for a chest infection, which progressed to a cardiac arrest under Beverly's care. No alarm monitors sounded when the baby stopped breathing, which baffled the nurses. The baby was put on life support, but his parents decided to pull the plug once it became apparent that their little boy would not survive.

From February to April of 1991, Beverly murdered four children and caused grievous bodily harm to many more. On May 28, 1993, she was convicted of four counts of murder, 11 counts of causing grievous bodily harm, and 11 counts of attempted murder. All of her crimes took place in the children's ward of Grantham and Kesteven Hospital in Lincolnshire. She is now serving 13 concurrent life sentences in the Rampton Secure Hospital of Nottinghamshire.

Another serial killer went by the name of Joseph Michael Swango. As an aspiring physician, Joseph Michael had direct access to his patients and colleagues. This allowed him to poison 60 people, but he was only convicted of the murder of four.

In 1983, Joseph Michael became a medical intern at the Ohio State University Medical Center (OSUMC). During his stay at the OSUMC, nurses noticed that healthy patients started dying spontaneously, for no apparent reason. An investigation ensued, but there was not enough evidence to convict Joseph Michael. While people were suspicious of him because he always seemed to be around when a death occurred, no one could provide proof that would stand up in court.

Nevertheless, his performance was bad enough that the OSUMC did not give him a resident position. In 1984, he therefore became an emergency medical technician with the Adams County Ambulance Corps. His coworkers there became suspicious of him when many of them started getting sick. They noticed a pattern—when they drank coffee that Joseph Michael had prepared, they became sick. At the same time, many patients were dying under Joseph Michael's care.

The former medical intern was arrested in 1985 for battery—i.e., poisoning his colleagues with arsenic and other toxins. He was sentenced to a mere five years of imprisonment. In 1989, he was released from prison and immediately resumed his killing spree, falsifying documents to get healthcare jobs. He was finally sentenced to life imprisonment in 1997, and is now jailed at the

ADX Florence Supermax Prison, where he will live out the remainder of his life.

Last but not least, Charles Cullen is another serial killer from the same mold as Donald Harvey. While Donald killed 87, Cullen is estimated to have killed around 400 people, making him a contender for the title of "Most Prolific Serial Killer." The problem is, there is a lack of proof.

Cullen committed his first murder in 1988 by giving John W. Wengo, Sr. an overdose of intravenous medicine. He went on to contaminate IV bags and poison more patients with other drugs (e.g. insulin). When the contaminated IVs were found and an investigation ensued, Cullen left St. Barnabas Hospital in search of a new job. When the hospital concluded that Cullen was behind the mysterious deaths, he was long gone.

He took many different jobs over the course of the next 15 years. He was employed at different hospitals as a nursing assistant, and he even became a nurse at a critical care unit. From 1988 to 2003, he used numerous different drugs and poisons to kill off his victims. One of his victims even reported that she saw a strange man inject something into her IV bag the night before, but relatives and other nurses discounted her story as an old woman's misunderstanding.

On December 15, 2003, Cullen was finally apprehended. In the end, he was convicted of only 35 murders, but he is suspected of committing up to 400. Aside from their shared disparity between murders and convictions, Cullen is similar to Donald Harvey in other ways as well. He too said that he killed because he could not bear to see the patients "code"—i.e., be declared a "code blue emergency." He ended their lives before more suffering ensued.

While Donald Harvey was a prolific hospital killer, he was not the only one—and apparently, not even the worst. Many other serial killers have plagued the medical profession, and there will doubtless be more in the future. We don't know whether to blame society or a chemical imbalance in the brain for their actions. What we do know is that now, more than ever, people should stay alert and aware, for no one knows who might be the next Angel of Death.

Epilogue

The worst crimes are sometimes committed with the best intentions. Donald Harvey was a serial killer—there is no doubt about it. But at times, he was able to trick himself into thinking that he was doing his victims a favor. He fooled himself into thinking that, even though he was committing murder, he was still doing the right thing.

Donald Harvey grew up in a disturbed household. He experienced abuse that no child ever should. His first nonconsensual sexual encounter came at the age of 4, and while there are many laws against pedophilia, no one cared enough to notice that Donald was being abused.

His parents were too busy fighting with each other to notice that their child was going through irreversible trauma. While other kids were experiencing childhood, Donald was learning how to survive in a cruel world.

Over the course of his life, he worked in three different hospitals as a nurse assistant or an orderly. He claimed to have killed around 87 people, but was only convicted of 37 murders. He attempted to kill and successfully harmed many more.

While Donald Harvey seemed like a regular guy with above-average smarts, he hid his disturbed childhood and various harrowing experiences behind fake smiles and a soft-spoken attitude. He charmed his way out of most of his troubles and got away with his crimes—until overconfidence gave him away.

The world is a cruel place to have produced a man like Donald Harvey. He died a death that many believe he deserved—and yet, did the world not make him who he was?

Also by Jack Smith

THE HAPPY FACE
MURDERER
The Life of Serial Killer Keith Hunter Jesperson
Jack Smith

THE HORRIFIC CRIMES
GILLES DE RAIS
REVISITED
Life of a Serial Killer of the Middle Ages
Jack Smith

THE BEAST OF
BIRKENSHAW
LIFE OF SERIAL KILLER
PETER MANUEL
JACK SMITH

BODIES
IN BARRELS
THE SNOWTOWN MURDERS
JACK SMITH

HIDDEN
BRUTALITY
LIFE OF SERIAL KILLER CARL EUGENE WATTS
JACK SMITH

THE SPOKANE
KILLER
The Life of Serial Killer Robert Lee Yates Jr.
Jack Smith

Most Mysterious and Headless Unsolved Murders of All Time
Five Gruesome Unsolved Mysteries
JACK SMITH

The Barton
MURDER
The Mysterious and True Murder Story on Hamilton Mountain. Did Someone Get Away With Murder?
Jack Smith

THE CROSS COUNTRY
KILLER
Life of Serial Killer Tommy Lynn Sells
Jack Smith